Ravel
According to
Ravel

Ravel
According to
Ravel

Vlado Perlemuter
and
Hélène Jourdan-Morhange

Translated by Frances Tanner
Edited by Harold Taylor

Kahn & Averill, London
Pro/Am Music Resources Inc., White Plains, NY, USA

First published in Lausanne in 1970
First English edition published by Kahn & Averill in 1988

British Library Cataloguing in Publication Data

Ravel, Maurice, *1875–1937*
    Ravel according to Ravel.
    1. French piano music. Ravel, Maurice,
    1875–1937
    I. Title   II. Perlemuter, Vlado
    III. Taylor, Harold, *1925–*   IV. Ravel
    d'apres Ravel.   *English*
    786.1'092'4

    ISBN 0-900707-94-1

First published in the United States in 1988
by Pro/Am Music Resources Inc
White Plains, NY 10606

    ISBN 0-912483-19-9

Typeset in Garamond by The Castlefield Press Ltd

Printed and bound in Great Britain by
Redwood Burn Limited, Trowbridge, Wiltshire.

Contents

Foreword

Quand Madame Jourdan-Morhange et moi avons écrit le résumé de notre dialogue fait à la Radio française, nous n'avons jamais pensé qu'il atteindrait un public qui ne soit pas seulement professionnel. Je me réjouis donc que, par cette traduction en langue anglaise, ce petit livre ait l'occasion d'être connu par les mélomaines anglais et de tout ceux qui s'interessent à la musique de Ravel.

Vlado Perlemuter
20 octobre 1987
Paris

Preface

The origins of this book lie in a series of programmes broadcast from Paris in 1950 by Radio Française, in which Vlado Perlemuter played all Ravel's compositions for piano solo and discussed them with Hélène Jourdan-Morhange who had devised the series. A transcript of their conversations was published three years later by Editions du Cervin, Lausanne, under the title *Ravel d'après Ravel*. It was Colette who suggested this title.

The book ran into four editions in its original form, but despite its importance the only translation it received was in 1969 into Japanese. An extra section, devoted to Ravel's two piano concertos, was added for the fifth edition, which appeared in 1970. In these conversations Perlemuter was interviewed by the publisher of the book, Pierre Maylan. It is from that edition that this first English translation has been prepared.

As Hélène Jourdan-Morhange explains in her opening remarks, the significance of the discussions lies in the fact that Vlado Perlemuter studied the whole of Ravel's solo piano music with the composer himself. This was in 1927 when Perlemuter was twenty-three years old. How this came about was described by the pianist when he was the subject of a BBC 'Desert Island Discs' radio programme and broadcast on the occasion of his eightieth birthday in 1984. He explained to the interviewer, Roy Plomley, how he was so "absolutely taken" by *Jeux d'eau*, the first piece by Ravel he had learned, that he simply had to go on and study all the others. Ravel, for his part, was so touched that a young pianist, at the outset of his career, had taken the time and trouble to learn all his piano music that he readily consented to coach him – once he had been approached.

Perlemuter confessed that as a "rather shy" young man he might never have written to the notoriously reclusive composer had it not been for the encouragement of one of his friends, Claude Crussard, the founder of the group *Ars Rediviva*.

The value of *Ravel According to Ravel* to pianists is obvious, but the comprehensive background notes which are woven into the conversational fabric give it a much wider appeal. Performers and listeners alike will find it a fascinating guide to the exploration of the magical sound-world of Ravel's piano music.

Through its publication we also pay tribute to another great French musician – Vlado Perlemuter, who has served for so many years not only Ravel, but the whole art of music, with unfailing devotion and integrity.

The Editor

Editorial Notes

Vlado Perlemuter, born in 1904, studied with Alfred Cortot at the Paris Conservatoire, where, after winning the 1st Prize in 1919 and the Prix d'Honneur in 1920 in his class, he won the Prix Diémer in 1921. Later, in 1951, he returned to the Conservatoire as Professor of Piano. In 1927 he studied all Ravel's solo piano works with the composer and played the complete œuvre in Paris in 1929. He is a pianist of international repute.

Hélène Jourdan-Morhange, born in 1892, was a violinist. She gave first performances of a number of Ravel works in 1922. Rheumatism put an end to her career. She was one of Ravel's closest friends in the last twenty years of his life. She was married to the artist Luc-Albert-Moreau and died in 1961.

All textual references are to the original editions, all published by Durand, Paris, except *Menuet Antique* (Enoch, Paris), *Pavane pour une infante défunte, Jeux d'eau* and *Miroirs* (Max Eschig, Paris) and *A la manière de . . .* (Salabert, Paris).

Vlado Perlemuter has recorded the following Ravel piano compositions on UK Nimbus and available only on compact disc:

NIM 5005   Gaspard de la Nuit
             Jeux d'eau
             Miroirs
             Pavane pour une Infante défunte

NIM 5011   A la manière de Borodine
             A la manière de Chabrier
             Menuet Antique
             Menuet sur le nom d'Haydn
             Prélude
             Sonatine
             Le Tombeau de Couperin
             Valses Nobles et Sentimentales

MENUET ANTIQUE
PAVANE POUR UNE INFANTE DÉFUNTE
JEUX D'EAU

Hêlêne Jourdan-Morhange I had the idea for these broadcasts while listening to a recital of works by Ravel performed by Vlado Perlemuter. Perlemuter is one of the few pianists who, not satisfied with having merely played some of Ravel's pieces to him, as so many others have done, really worked at the whole piano output with the Maestro. It seemed a pity that such a testament should reach only a limited concert public.

For six months, several times a week, Perlemuter took the train to Montfort l'Amaury, where he met Ravel in his little country house. In that tiny, dark blue study whose décor I have so often recalled, with its little gothic objects placed next to the dolls, clockwork birds and divers in bottles – in this little study they used to work together, Ravel explaining to Vlado why he had written one particular bit, how another should be interpreted, why the quizzical smile must sometimes stifle lyrical ardour, how to weave supernatural sounds around fairies and gnomes. The Maestro would voice his slightest whims – I ought to say: his slightest wishes, for I have never known a composer so sure of himself with regard to the markings in his music. So Ravel used to say everything that had to be done, but above all . . . what was not to be done. No worldly kindness restrained him when he was giving his opinion. The story of *Bolero* conducted by Toscanini is well known: "That's much too fast" Ravel told him after the performance. Toscanini took the remark very badly! Ravel had not realised that some conductors are beyond criticism!

After all the hours spent discussing as much as playing the piano, it could be said that Vlado Perlemuter is one of the custodians of Ravel's thought. No-one can play more like Ravel. Having worked on the *Sonata*, the *Duo* and the *Trio* with Ravel when I was a violinist, I recognise in Perlemuter's interpretations all the idiosyncracies, all Ravel's wishes: exaggerated swells, crescendi which explode in anger, turns which die on a clear note, the gentle friction of affectionate cats . . . and in all this fantasy, strict time in expression and rigour even in rubato.

That is why, finding myself confronted by this marvel of an interpretation absolutely faithful to the tradition of the composer, I asked Vlado Perlemuter if he would come to the microphone and enlighten many musicians who, gradually, without wanting to, lose touch with the tradition of Ravel. So in several sessions and piece by piece, we will study Ravel's piano works, illustrating what should be done and also what should not be done.

MENUET ANTIQUE

H J-M The *Menuet Antique* is the composer's first published work. Dating from 1895, it is dedicated to his friend and first interpreter, Ricardo Vinès. It is the period when Ravel, still at the Conservatoire, impressed masters and pupils by his unassuming personality. They were astounded to be present at the blooming of an orchid in their field of daisies!

Ravel used to play the *Gymnopédies* of Satie and the *Valses Romantiques* by Chabrier from memory. And this is the point I wanted to make: Chabrier's contribution to the development of the young Ravel. Ravel recognised it himself. It is obvious that the *Menuet Antique* was inspired by the *Menuet Pompeux* which Ravel, in fact, was to orchestrate later, in 1918.

PAVANE POUR UNE INFANTE DEFUNTE

H J-M Ravel did not like this piece very much. In an article he wrote in 1912, when he was a music critic, about a concert in which the *Pavane* was played, he said: "By an irony of fate, the first work which I must review is my own *Pavane pour une Infante Défunte*. I don't feel too embarrassed to talk about it; it is old enough for the composer to hand over to the critic. I no longer see its good points from such a distance. But, alas, I perceive its faults very clearly: the glaring influence of Chabrier and the rather poverty-stricken form! The remarkable interpretation of this incomplete and unoriginal work contributed, I think, to its success." You can't be more objective than that!

Vlado, did Ravel give you any advice about this Pavane?

Vlado Perlemuter No. When I brought it to him, he pulled a face and said: "Oh, have you been studying that?" He wasn't interested.

H J-M We all know that he did not want it to be played too slowly, according to the anecdote told by Charles Oulmont. When he was very young, Charles Oulmont played this *Pavane* to Ravel, too slowly, which brought about this observation from the amused composer: "Watch out, little one, it's not a Pavane défunte pour une Infante!"

Ravel must have liked your interpretation, since he made no comment.

JEUX D'EAU

H J-M And now, with *Jeux d'eau*, we return to the task we assigned ourselves; attempting to discover for musicians Ravel's true wishes.

Jeux d'eau dates from 1901. That is when Ravel and his friends — 'The Apaches' as they called their group — gathered several times a week at the home of the painter Paul Sordes. Vinès, Delarge, Fargue, Calvocoressi, Vuillermoz and others were there. They used to discuss literature as well as music, and that is where each one brought, still panting, his latest creation. Ravel offered the first hearing of *Jeux d'eau* to his 'Apache' companions. "There was", writes Fargue, "a strange fire, a whole panoply of subtleties and vibrations which none of us could previously have imagined." Indeed, this piece opens up new horizons in piano technique, especially if one remembers that Debussy's *Jardins sous la pluie* was not written until two years later, in 1903.

Can you tell us Ravel's main comments?

V P He wanted the opening not too fast, but without dragging. Melodic but not sentimental. The theme is cheerful and gentle, not brisk. We mustn't forget the inscription, taken from Henri de Regnier: "River god laughing as the water tickles him." The way to produce the necessary floating sonority is to keep a light hand, but with the fingers close to the keys.

H J-M It is often played quite articulated.

V P Indeed, that is because it is difficult to obtain the necessary fluidity when it is slurred, but notwithstanding, Ravel asked me to play the beginning smoothly and legato.

Here is something important: here (Ex 1) the group of grace notes must not be inserted in the bar, but must fall between the two bars.

H J-M One must not forget the little comma which one meets so often in Ravel's works, in different contexts. As you have underlined in your performance, it restores the importance of the beginning of the melody.

V P After the exposition of the second theme, there is a tendency to make a cadenza in the style of Liszt. At this point, Ravel told me: "Let it move, but don't hurry." (Ex 2.)

Here, (Ex 3) the figuration is often integrated with the melody. On the contrary, these two elements should be kept well apart.

H J-M The pianist must not ape a tenor showing off his command of passage work!

V P This phrase continues in an immense crescendo and *here* you mustn't be afraid of making it sound like Liszt!

H J-M It is really interesting to note that already in *Jeux d'eau*, Ravel's first important piece, the early signs can be found of that immense crescendo which in Ravel's music is like the explosion of his modesty which has been repressed too long; the confession which bursts out of his music and releases all the passion of *Daphnis*, the fatal frenzy of *La Valse* or the measured freedom of *Bolero*. Ricardo Vinès told me that Ravel advocated the use of the pedal in high passages, in order to give the blurred impression of vibrations in the air, rather than distinct notes.

V P Yes, he wanted the concluding figuration to be hazy in order to let the left hand sing through (Ex 4).

There is also a controversy about the end of *Jeux d'eau*. Many pianists slow down the final arpeggio as if the water were slowly draining away (Ex 5). Ravel wanted the end to be arrived at through shading; a kind of question mark. . . .

SONATINE

H J-M We will follow the chronological order of Ravel's piano works. Today we tackle the *Sonatine* which dates from 1905 so it is still a work in his early style, still rich in its velvet harmonies. Ravel is not yet worried about keeping up his reputation and lets his muse run free. His feeling for harmony, his new chords do not stop him from giving the *Sonatine* a classical structure (*Sonatine* because of its modest dimensions) and even a cyclic character, since the opening theme recurs in the *Menuet* and in some passages in the *Final*.   The spontaneity of youth bursts out, just as it does in the *Quartet* of four years earlier! It is impossible not to be won over by this surging melody, this writing so unfettered that it is not afraid of the constraints of the classical design. Ravel is in his element in this youthful work. So unfavourably inclined towards his early works, he did not disown the *Sonatine*, because he played it when on tour in America instead of the *Concerto in G* which was intended for that occasion, but which he abandoned at the last moment, finding it too difficult. When the pianist Robert Schmitz, who was then in America, urged him to play it, he replied: "I am not a pianist and I don't want to be exhibited as if I were in a circus!" So he played his *Sonatine* and accompanied some songs. . . .

I have often heard the first part of the *Sonatine* played too fast. What do you think?

V P Indeed, it is nearly always played too fast. Ravel insisted that the tempo should not be too hurried.

H J-M Besides, as always with Ravel, there is an indication on the score. Here it is – 'modéré'. Will you now tell us what were Ravel's main wishes?

V P Apart from the tempo, which Ravel wanted to be strict and without rubato, he was very concerned about the exact length of the semiquaver in the second theme (Ex 6):

The semiquaver must not be played with expression; if it is 'interpreted' it becomes weak and loses the rhythm which Ravel wanted.

H J-M In fact, it is the little comma before the semiquaver which gives it its impetus; moreover, the diminuendo which precedes it demands this comma, it being no longer a matter of score-reading, but a question of interpretation.

V P At the melody marked 'very expressive' but *ppp*, we enter the area in Ravel's output which demands great independence in dynamics (Ex 7). We find this much more developed in *Miroirs* and above all in *Le Gibet*.

H J-M In the passage which acts as the conclusion of the exposition, where Ravel borrows the first notes of the theme, there is a quaver which you lean on like a sigh. Is that intended? (Ex 8)

V P It is marked! There is a 'hairpin' and it is never made enough of. Also, these signs are found again at the end of the first piece. Here (Ex 9) the melody stands out. After this melody, Ravel wanted a slight break after the very slight rallentando which he asked me to make. Likewise in the recapitulation.

Menuet

H J-M In the *Menuet*, once again it is a question of tempo. Ravel used to say: "Generally, it is played too spikily." He wanted it to be quite slow, didn't he?

V P Slow but moving, and above all, with great exactitude of rhythm.

H J-M What did Ravel recommend?

V P He asked me, above all, to play it sensitively, but not over-refined.

H J-M The great difficulty in Ravel is to play sensitively without being dragged into *rubato*. He told Ricardo Vinès: "Avoid emphasising the first beat; that would be vulgar. . . ."

V P Before the reprise, both aspects of the theme are brought together. Ravel insisted on the left hand being very expressive. Moreover, he marked it in, yet pianists take little notice of it (Ex 10).

Just before the return of the theme, the chromatic notes will be lightly stressed, and the repeat arrived at without slowing down (Ex 11).

H J-M Slowing down is anti-Ravelian! Not slowing down doesn't mean playing inflexibly. Ravel's strict approach doesn't scorn subtlety. We see here what will often prove to be the case, that subtlety in bringing in repeats is not achieved by slowing down but through sonority.

The end is a kind of Pavane, isn't it?

V P Yes. Ravel told me: "It's very broad . . . like a deep curtsey. . . ." (See p. 7, last four bars.)

H J-M But how do you manage not to blur the harmonies whilst holding down the pedal?

V P There you have pinpointed something which is a guide-line for Ravel's music as well as that of Debussy: a light vibration of the foot on the pedal which, if successful, allows a bass note to be held through the changes of harmony. They quickly die away, leaving the bass note sounding at the end.

Final

H J-M And now, let's discuss the tempo of the *Final*.

V P Ravel wanted it to be very fast, but not rushed. It's not solely a piece of virtuosity.

H J-M Yes, the piece contains a violent passion.

V P The danger of rushing is all the greater in that this movement is very difficult. At the beginning, the *agité* must be brought out by the 'hairpin', but without rushing the tempo (Ex 12).

H J-M There is one thing which can't be emphasised enough: the relationship of the rallentando to the preceding and following tempi.

V P It is essential in Ravel, but it also exists in other composers, Schumann in particular. Take the first movement of this *Sonatine* and also the *Final*, for example. I have a pupil who can never manage to grade his rallentandi (see page 9, fourth stave).

H J-M In the phrase marked 'very soft and expressive' I find that the sound is never ethereal enough.

V P It is a question of touch. Many pianists attack from too high, whereas the fingers must remain in yielding contact with the keys. The accent should be obtainable by pressure, not by articulation (see page 9, line 5, bar 4 etc).

H J-M And the horn passage? Should it be brought out?

V P Of course; in spite of the pianissimo, Ravel wanted the re-appearance of the theme to sound like a horn fanfare. "Rather brassy", he said (Ex 13).

H J-M And a lot of expression in the melodic phrases, in spite of the myth about Ravel's dryness?

V P The leading theme, which is also that of the first movement, must be very expressive. The left hand should be very singing. Pianists rarely play it like that (Ex 14).

H J-M Have you any more points to make?

V P After the bit marked '*retenu*' he wanted a sudden return to the initial tempo (see page 12, line 4, bars 1 and 2). At the '*très animé*' of the ending, at the spot marked '*très marqué*', Ravel asked me to return to *piano*, in order to finish with more éclat (see page 15, line 3).

H J-M I seem to remember that there is another little pedalling trick at the end?

V P Yes, before making the final flourish, the pedal should be held whilst you take your breath . . . in short, you breathe during the pedal in order to let the final chord sparkle (Ex 15).

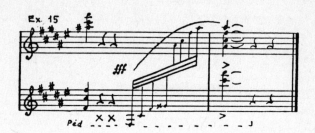

MIROIRS:

Noctuelles
Oiseaux Tristes
Une Barque sur l'Océan
Alborada del Gracioso
La Vallée des Cloches

H J-M It was also at the meetings, already mentioned, of the 'Apaches' that Ravel revealed to his friends his piano pieces gathered together in one collection: *Miroirs*. After the *Quartet, Jeux d'eau* and the triumph of *Schéhérazade*, Ravel did not wish to rest on his laurels. Still hard on himself, he wanted to renew his style. "*Miroirs*", he writes, "marked a change in my harmonic development which was great enough to disconcert even those most accustomed to my style up to that point."

The five pieces of *Miroirs: Noctuelles, Oiseaux Tristes, Une Barque sur l'Océan, Alborada del Gracioso,* and *La Vallée des Cloches*, are dedicated to L-P Fargue, Vinès, Sordes, Calvocoressi, and Maurice Delarge. These important pages mark a definite stage, the stage which could be called impressionist, a word which is attached too often and mistakenly to all his music. Here, each image is drawn with a lively, firm touch; straightforward painting which is far removed from the symbolism of Debussy.

Noctuelles

Noctuelles is completely fluid . . . hazy sounds, birds flying, seeking one another. . . . One could believe that Ravel was inspired by something written by his friend Fargue, to whom the work is dedicated: "The moths leave the cart-sheds in awkward flight, to cling to other beams."

As in *Jeux d'eaux*, Ravel was inspired by Liszt, and above all, by *Feux follets*! What were Ravel's comments?

V P He insisted very much on the little crescendo and diminuendo 'hairpins' returning to their starting point (see page 3). Here, (see page 4, line 5, bars 2 and 3) he wanted the melody to be full of colour and a certain inner liveliness.

H J-M Altogether, another interpretation in the style of Liszt!

V P He wanted this bar (Ex 16) to sound like a gust of wind between the others which are expressive and sustained.

H J-M The crescendo goes from pianissimo to forte in a single bar, foreshadowing the outbursts of *scarbo*.

V P At the *rubato* which precedes the *lento*, Ravel asked me to bring out the accents in the left hand (see page 5, line 4, bars 2 and 3), and that is why the rubato is necessary . . . so that the triple rhythm takes its place calmly beneath the duple rhythm of the right hand, a subtle way of introducing the rubato.

H J-M In fact, its a rubato à la Chopin, that's to say: a rubato which doesn't distort the rhythm.

V P There is also the cadence preceding the *lento* which should be played with great fluidity (see page 5, last line).

H J-M And now we arrive at the slow passage which, for me, contains potentially the whole of *Le Gibet* from *Gaspard de la Nuit*. Have you any advice to give about it?

V P There is the pedal note – dominant of the relative minor – which must be vibrant at the beginning, then fade to become only a vibration, so that the theme may be played according to Ravel's marking: 'sombre and expressive' – which to my mind is the most inspiring suggestion that one can make (see page 6, first 3 lines).

H J-M After the expressive phrase, the changeability of Ravel's mood should be demonstrated; the pirouette after sadness. Here, it is represented by an arabesque from *Noctuelles*.
    The end seems to me to resemble the style of Liszt even more.

V P It's a cadenza which could certainly appear in Liszt's *Feux Follets* (see page 11, last two lines). Out of the duality of the two elements which lead in the recapitulation, there emerges a particularly rich pianistic complexity whose lyricism should be emphasised.

H J-M So much for those who find Ravel dry!

Oiseaux Tristes

H J-M Let's pass on to *Oiseaux Tristes*. It is said that whilst Ravel was walking in the forest, he was inspired by the song of a blackbird and that he heard this page in the drowsy heat of a summer morning. Did Ravel make any special points?

V P There are three which are still very clear in my mind. The first concerns the arabesque of the sad bird, which must not be played strictly in time, but more briskly (Ex 17). Ravel himself wrote it on my music. If you play strictly what's written, it loses character. You must not be afraid of lingering on the long note. As soon as you compress the outline of this arabesque, it stands out.

H J-M Yes, like a bird in the sky. Vinès used to say: "It's a Japanese print." What is the second remark Ravel made?

V P Perhaps this observation was meant only for me, but I think many pianists could benefit from it; those who might, as I did, interpret Ravel's *Lent ad libitum* too much according to the letter. The *Lent* refers only to the chord and the prolongation of that chord before one sets off again quite rapidly on the cadenza (see page 15, bar 1).

H J-M In fact, we find again the same kind of tautness which Ravel wanted in the arabesque at the beginning. And the third point?

V P The third point is extremely subtle. In the last four bars, the conclusion of the piece, there are some chords over which accents appear and which are often obscured by the non-chord tones. Ravel wanted the chords to dominate completely. The great problem is that the other notes should nevertheless be heard sounding in the distance (Ex 18).

H J-M If the pianist succeeds in bringing off this subtle effect he will have achieved the wish of Ravel who wanted this passage to sound "sombre and distant".

Une Barque sur l'Océan

H J-M And now let us consider the third piece of *Miroirs*. It is the only piece in the *Miroirs* which has no metronome marking. Ravel did not trust the swell of the ocean!

V P Moreover, it is simply marked: 'with supple rhythm'.

H J-M What are your comments?

V P Ravel asked me to play the beginning "without hurrying and not too fast", so that the piece doesn't become a springboard for virtuosity. The time signature 6/8, 2/4 demonstrates to what extent Ravel wanted the suppleness of coupled rhythms.

H J-M I find this piece particularly orchestral.

V P But Ravel orchestrated it! He wasn't satisfied with it, however, but it proves that he could hear sounds in it containing orchestral colour. Listen to the passage (Ex 19), where you must bring out the theme. Surely it's orchestral? He told me: "Softly, but like a bugle call".

H J-M Further on there is another orchestral effect which makes one think of kettle drums.

V P Here are the kettle drums (Ex 20) and also the brassy sonority of the left hand (Ex 21), a passage of unique grandeur in Ravel's work. In the passage where the swell of the ocean is repeated three times, Ravel asked me to make a tiny pause before each wave, right up to the end of the piece.

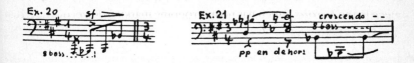

H J-M Continuing our orchestral researches, I spotted a pretty harp effect at the end (Ex 22).

V P In fact, Ravel wrote on my score: "Like a harp".

H J-M How did he want the end to sound?

V P The end is particularly interesting; the impression of a rallentando is created by the context of the composition. It is self-made by the skilful rhythmic notation. So it is pointless to slow down in reality.

H J-M It's rather like the procedure of Honegger in *Pacific 231*. He obtains a rallentando by augmentation, and on the contrary, an acceleration by a diminution of the note values.

Alborada del Gracioso

H J-M The works inspired by Spain renewed in some measure the style of the composer. They led Ravel to react, after his first compositions, against an impressionism from which he wanted to free himself. Thus in the *Miroirs*, after *Noctuelles, Oiseaux Tristes* and *Une Barque sur l'Océan*, which are all permeated with reflections of sky and sea, *Alborada* arrives like a meteor from its colourful country of origin, with its lashing accents and 'earthy' rhythms.

V P It's quite a unique piece in Ravel's works and perhaps the most difficult because of its precision and its technical demands.

H J-M At the very beginning, did Ravel have any particular comments for you?

V P Yes, he wanted each chord to be very taut, like a guitar being plucked, and in a lively tempo.

H J-M Hm! That's a rather dangerous piece of advice for certain pianists who have a craze for speed.

V P It has to be said, however, for those who, on the contrary, might tend to be too cautious; their caution occasioned by the difficulty of the work.

H J-M It's also a useful comment with regard to the steadiness of the tempo, which mustn't vary.

V P Yes, if you don't play it quickly enough, you are apt to hurry this passage.

H J-M I would like to hear that little crescendo, that kind of 'hairpin' which is so typical of Ravel, which I don't often hear in performances.

V P Here it is. It is difficult in that the two chords are detached (Ex 23), so the first one must be *piano* in order to give the impulse to the second. In the recapitulation it is easier because the first chord is broken and slurred

V P As an example of a precise indication, Ravel wanted me to play this passage (Ex 25) lightly, like a flautist, recalling the orchestra.

H J-M In the *Aubade*, after the opening phrase, Ravel has marked a return to the first tempo. Now, I have quite often heard pianists hurry this passage.

V P For once Ravel's marking: quaver = quaver must be interpreted, since he specifically asked me to play it with a remote sound and not too fast (Ex 26). He said it was like a distant murmuring.

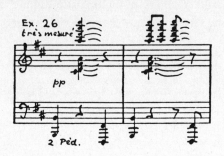

H J-M Of course the lyrical passages must be extremely lyrical?

V P Unfortunately for these passages, the high register of the piano is less accommodating than when one is writing for the orchestra, where expressive quality is much more easily displayed at these pitches.

H J-M And how do you play your *glissandi*?

V P I use Ravel's fingering: 4–2 going up, 3–1 coming down. But it goes without saying that each pianist will have his own fingering. Ravel was prestigious in *glissandi* in double notes, but that was probably due to the shape of his thumb!

H J-M Yes, that rather square-ended thumb which enabled him to produce drum-like sonorities in the *Sonata for Violin and Piano*.

V P Moreover, Ravel preferred a good single-note *glissando* to a bad double-note one. The important thing was to give the impression of a rapid spurt ending with an accent (see page 41, line 2, first bar). At the end, the third-beat accents must not slow down the movement (see page 44, line 4, third bar etc).

La Vallée des Cloches

H J-M And now, let's pass on to *La Vallée des Cloches*, with its melancholy fervour, and whose sustained melody is as long as that of the *Piano Concerto*.

V P One must pay great attention to the marking at the beginning: very soft and un-accented; a sonerous, melting atmosphere. The metronome speed requested by Ravel is very good, but it calls for great independence between the hands.

H J-M Must the three different bells be equally clear?

V P More exactly, they must superimpose themselves with differing sonorities, each one having its own character (Ex 27).

Before embarking on the second idea (see page 46, line 2, second bar), you should let the sounds carry on and underline the organ point which Ravel wants by keeping the pedal down. Let go of it at the moment the *Très calme* begins.

H J-M In this so calm and beautiful theme, don't you find that there is a tendency to hurry?

V P Yes, unfortunately; this stems from the simplicity of the theme. What is required is to clothe it with the poetry which it inspires in oneself. All is ruined if one hurries.

H J-M And this calmness brings us to the broadest example of lyricism we can ever find in Ravel (Ex 28).

In the last four bars, I seem to hear the great bell of Boris Godunov.

V P In fact Ravel asked for a big accent on the last and new big bell, more sonorous than might be imagined from the *vif* indicated (Ex 29). Furthermore, it is this bell which announces the conclusion of the piece.

GASPARD DE LA NUIT

Ondine
Le Gibet
Scarbo

MENUET SUR LE NOM D'HAYDN

H J-M Ravel got to know *Gaspard de la Nuit* through Ricardo Vinès. Few composers knew the poet, Aloysius Bertrand, a strange romatic figure from that time when fairy-tale Gothic was in fashion. Already attracted to Edgar Allen Poe, Ravel was to be tempted by this tormented poet who took pleasure in the infernal visions of the Middle Ages. Aloysius Bertrand cut his poetic gems into thousands of facets. One can imagine how this "goldsmith of words", as Sainte-Beuve called him, conquered our goldsmith of sounds! The three poems chosen by Ravel are quite dissimilar, but because of their perfect musical realisation, they seem to have been intentionally gathered together by the poet. The structure is almost that of a sonata: *Allegro, Adagio* and a dazzling *Finale.*

Ondine

V P Ravel didn't want *Ondine* to be played too slowly. He wanted it to be very melodic, very expressive, very soft and tender. He wrote: "faster, more melting" all over my score.

H J-M In *Ondine* there are those famous rubatos of Ravel which are rubatos 'in time', in spite of their flexibility.

V P Ravel wrote on my music: "indicate the rhythm of the triplet with suppleness".

H J-M That's extremely difficult, for within a multitude of nuances, you have to keep the unity of time which was one of Ravel's tenets.

V P Yes, if you slow down, it becomes a subdivided rhythm, whereas it should always keep going (see page 6, line 2, bar 1).

H J-M Have you any more details to give us?

V P Yes, at this point (Ex 30), he wanted continuity in the melody in spite of the inflexions.

Ex. 30

Also, before the recitative which precedes the ending, there is a pause which is usually made too long. Ravel didn't want it to become a piece within a piece and above all, he didn't want it to slow down (Ex 31).

Ex. 31

H J-M In the ending, don't we have the Ravelian false rallentando of which we have already spoken in connection with *Une Barque sur l'Ocean*?

V P Yes, Ravel marked on my score: "rallentando by augmentation" which to his mind meant allowing the movement to slow down through its notation. If it's done properly, I would call it a real rallentando (see page 14, end of second line and third line). I would also like to mention that at the beginning of the cadenza, Ravel asked me to start the arpeggio immediately, without any holding back on the two grace notes which might be construed as notes to be leaned on (see the beginning of page 14).

H J-M And the end?

V P Ravel asked me to play *non-legato*, recalling the pulsations of the opening (see page 14, last two lines).

Le Gibet

In its starkness, *Le Gibet* is hallucinatory with its unchanging, muffled and continuous pedal: a fatal bell which dies away in the gloom of the final *pianissimo*. In this single page, Ravel has translated all the macabre resonance of the poem whose final sentence explains it: "It is the bell which tolls on the walls of the town, beneath the horizon, and the carcass of a hanged man reddened by the setting sun".

I think, Vlado, that *Le Gibet* is one of your favourite pieces by Ravel?

V P Yes, I admire it very much, but perhaps it is one of the most complicated pieces to play because you must not be afraid of making it sound monotonous.

H J-M It is like a great classical *adagio* where you must not be afraid of wearying the public, otherwise you begin to hurry.

V P It all depends on one's inner capacity. In *Le Gibet* the haunting repetition of the bell must be unchanging from beginning to end.

H J-M What did Ravel have to say?

V P Ravel insisted on absolutely strict tempo. The grandeur of the piece depends on the rhythmical structure. It is not simply a bell swinging; Ravel asked for the 'scaffold' theme (Ex 32) to be well marked, but without expression, whereas the answer (Ex 33) should be very *cantabile*.

H J-M It must be very difficult to produce all these different sonorities with only two hands.

V P Indeed, it is necessary to have complete control of the keyboard. Thus in this expressive passage, both hands play in unison with the sonority of the bell and at the same time with another sonority for the additional note which forms the chord.

H J-M In short, we are joining up with the great polyphonic technique of Bach! Is there a rule about playing in unison?

V P Yes, the left hand must be only an echo of the right.

Here, when you arrive at this extraordinary complexity of sounds (bars 20–26), above all, don't slow down, in spite of the difficulty of joining up the chords, which in spite of their unusual spread, must be played very *legato*, as Ravel marked (see page 18, line 2, bar 2 etc).

H J-M In spite of the strictness which Ravel demands in the whole piece, it seems to me that, all the same, there is one phrase whose pathos might advantageously be brought out? (Ex 34)

V P Actually, no. The pathos of the phrase, which is real, only takes on its whole grandeur when one observes exactly the intransigence of Ravel; he indicated: "a little marked, but without expression".

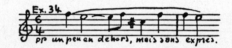

H J-M The curious thing is that this phrase, played in a slipshod manner, becomes a parody of Puccini!

V P That is why you must provide the expressive intensity in strict time.

H J-M And that's difficult! I admire the way you manage to keep that unified expressiveness which gives pathos to the whole piece. And at the end?

V P As always, don't slow down. This marvellous ending is obtained by sonority and not by slowing down. The phrase must melt into the *pianissimo*.

Scarbo

H J-M Now let's go on to *Scarbo*, the last piece in the triptych. After the static picture of *Le Gibet*, the little dwarf, Scarbo, appears even more frantic by comparison. You know what Ravel wrote to one of his friends: "I wanted to write a more difficult piece than *Islamey*"!

V P And he stuck to his guns! He expected a flawless performance of the score and that requires a transcendental technique.

H J-M Apparently, in writing this piece, the craftsman Ravel thought: "pure technique", but the hidden flame within him sprang to life – a flame so powerful that it scorns any denial by those in whom it lives! So *Scarbo* oddly exceeds the intentions of its composer.

V P And one mustn't forget this. Virtuosity is essential, but it is not an end! When I worked at *Scarbo* with the master, he told me: "I wanted to make a caricature of romanticism", then lowering his voice, he added: "but perhaps I let myself be taken over by it".

H J-M I find the essence of Ravel in that honesty towards himself. In any case, that sentence gives the interpreter the precise character of the piece.

V P And in spite of its apparent extravagance, what perfection there is in the form!

H J-M This is not the first time that Ravel arrives at classicality by the pathways of fantasy!

What have you to show us amongst so much splendour?

V P The first three notes at the beginning contain the essential theme of *Scarbo* in a nutshell. Ravel wrote on my music: "like a double bassoon" and then: "like a side drum" (Ex 35).

The theme of *Scarbo* is an enormous romantic outburst (Ex 36).

From the rhythmic point of view, many of the first beats are often played too feebly. The first beat is the springboard for the semiquaver (Ex 37).

H J-M The absence of the first beat undermines the sturdiness of the passage.

V P He wanted very explosive 'hairpins' throughout, not only those that are needed for the sake of expression (Ex 38), but also those in the left hand (see page 33, line 1, fifth and following bars).

At this spot (Ex 39), Ravel told me: "like kettledrums".

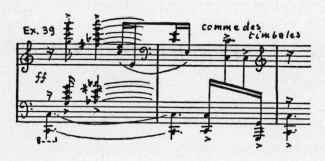

H J-M What with the double bassoon, side drum and kettle drums, we are confronted with a veritable orchestra!

V P Precisely, my friend. Ravel was very attached to the orchestral effects in this piece.

H J-M I recognise in all this the paradoxical nature of our dear Ravel. He orchestrates piano pieces such as *Alborada, Valses Nobles et Sentimentales* and *Le Tombeau de Couperin*, yet *Scarbo*, in which he advocates orchestral effects, he does not orchestrate!

V P He wanted to do the opposite. He said to me, in a slightly bantering tone: "I wanted to make an orchestral transcription for the piano!"

H J-M He must have imagined it played by an orchestra when he conceived it.

V P In the ascending chromatic seconds he wanted an enormous amount of pedal (see page 37, line 2, bar 1 etc). It should be very muffled, the *pianissimo* coming from very far away in order to save up the brilliant *crescendo* leading to the final episode. Here again, the *crescendo* is never made big enough (see page 39, last line, bar 5).

H J-M Again, it's the somewhat melodramatic effect of the black dog Belzébuth in *Noël des Jouets* or the Beast in *Ma Mère L'Oye*.

V P At the end, when the romantic theme reaches its climax, the master wrote on my music: "stormy" (Ex 40).

H J-M That reminds us of his weakness for Liszt! And the ending?

V P Ravel marked "faster" for me. Was it because I was playing it too slowly? In any case, it throws light on Ravel's intentions. He did not want the ending to be too slow, and once again, he marked over the last four bars: "Don't slow down".

H J-M The *Menuet* was written for the *Revue S.I.M.* (The Journal of the International Society for Musicology) in 1909; an edition devoted to the Haydn centenary. Ravel decided to write a minuet on the letters of Haydn's name. We know that Ravel liked a framework; playing around with a theme of which the notes were already specified was bound to appeal to him. At any rate, this dictated to him this charming minuet, a dance which is often found in his works. To make a courtly bow in a 'new look' jacket and a butterfly bow-tie fully satisfied his taste for paradox! The formality is there, but the little passing note slides in clandestinely to bring a little acid to the gesture!

V P Here are the notes based on Haydn's name; Ravel enjoyed the game and played it back to front and upside down (Ex 41).

H J-M Vlado, did you study this minuet with Ravel?

V P That would be an exaggeration. I simply played it to him, for the work did not appear to have much importance for him.

H J-M All the same, have you any comments to give us?

V P As in the minuet in the *Sonatine*, the marking is: 'Mouvement de Menuet', that's to say: graceful, moving along, but not fast. And as in *Le Tombeau de Couperin*, the grace notes should be on the beat and very incisive.

H J-M Should the 'precious' side be exaggerated?

V P I don't think that this written, constructed improvisation demands too much preciosity, however, the harmonies are typically Ravelian. In the middle of the piece there is a kind of bridge where the first two letters of the name are used to support a chromatic ascent (Ex 42). Ravel wrote on my copy: "mysterious and muffled".

H J-M And the end?

V P The last time the name appeared, Ravel asked me to play it "softly and lightly emphasised" (Ex 43).

VALSES NOBLES ET SENTIMENTALES

H J-M Let's leave that minor work in order to attack the *Valses Nobles et Sentimentales*, one of the most characteristic works in the Ravelian manner.

In 1910, when it was 'good form' to be an aesthete, the *Valses* brought with them a world of refined novelties. Ravel was still under the influence of Mallarmé, and let's not forget the motto of Henri de Regnier placed as an inscription above the title of the *Valses*: "The delicious and ever-changing pleasure of a useless occupation". It clearly indicates the spirit of the moment and the easy-going life of that epoch.

Ravel wrote: "The title of *Valses Nobles et Sentimentales* adequately conveys my intention of composing a chain of waltzes following the example of Schubert. The virtuosity which was the basis of *Gaspard de la Nuit* is succeeded by writing which is distinctly more transparent, giving more firmness to the harmonies and showing up the contours of the music in more relief".

Roland-Manuel finds in these waltzes the essential elements of Ravel's chord system. "Ravel created in them", he says, "a kind of reservoir on which his later works would draw frequently". It's the subtlety of these new harmonies which must have caused Debussy to say: "That's the finest ear which has ever existed".

I think, Vlado, that studying these waltzes with Ravel made the biggest impression on your memory?

V P In spite of the years which have passed, I can only be moved when I recall Ravel in his study, near the piano, score in hand, making me work at these waltzes. I have never seen so much intentness in his look, there was about him such a longing to be understood, to let nothing pass, not only textually, but in the interpretation of this text. Through the desire for perfection in the letter, one automatically made contact with the spirit.

H J-M I can see him so well, sifting through his score, picking out the note or nuance which might have led you astray from the text as it stood. It proves to what extent Ravel was attached to his *Valses*.

V P He was also anxious that the speed of each waltz should be marked on the programme.

H J-M Probably because it expresses the feeling with which each waltz should be interpreted. The first is marked *Modéré – Très franc* (moderate – very free), the second *Assez lent avec une expression intense* (very slowly with intense expression), the third *Modéré*, the fourth *Assez animé* (very lively).

FIRST WALTZ

V P The first waltz poses three problems: speed, pedalling and sonority.

H J-M Let's start with the rhythm. Of course it is not as fast as it is usually played?

V P Exactly. Moreover the metronome speed is marked by Ravel, but you must keep it on the lively side, not wildly so, but moving. Furthermore, with constant duality of duple and triple rhythms it becomes muddled if you rush it.

H J-M Will you give us an example of duple and triple?

V P Ravel made me repeat this one ten times with hands separate (Ex 44)! He was so fussy about getting it right. The chord on the third beat must not be squashed down.

H J-M I understand . . . for we violinists it is an up-bow so that the attack is less hard and the chord is thrown off.

V P That brings us to deploring the kind of brutality with which this waltz is often treated. Strength is needed, and tone, but not hardness.

H J-M What I call a bear-hug! You were talking just now about the extent of the sonority; did you want to mention the pedal?

V P I did want to mention the pedal. In fact it was the first time that Ravel really made me study the pedal. He thought that it was essential for these waltzes. You must not use any pedal for the chord on the third beat, but only on the first beat. In general, use short pedals to underline the rhythm.

H J-M And as the rhythms are lop-sided, the pedal must be used very delicately. A certain brilliant dryness, without hardness, is necessary.

V P Here (Ex 45), he wanted the leaning on the second beat in the left hand to be well marked.

Here (Ex 46), the melodic left hand accentuates its duple rhythm. Ravel very much wanted this to stand out.

H J-M I see written on the music: "not so loud", so once again one must conform to Ravel's wishes.

SECOND WALTZ

H J-M Will you give us some comments on the second waltz?

V P There is a tendency to drag it a little. It is obviously one of the *Valses sentimentales*, but it shouldn't be excessively slow.

H J-M Slowness always spoils the continuity of the curve of the melody.

H J-M Continuity of line in a shading which holds it together. Ravel never found this *crescendo–diminuendo* 'hairpin' projected enough.

H J-M Don't you find that after the accented preparation, one expects something . . . like the beginning of the *Grande Valse*, where the theme grows out of the anticipation?

V P The second time this kind of introduction appears, it introduces a new episode which is marked, extraordinarily for Ravel: *rubato* (Ex 47).

H J-M Rubato for Ravel is always in time. Ricardo Vinès used to say: "Since Ravel liked exact interpretations, he created a precisely placed rubato: the graded rubato.".

V P Here, it is more a hesitation in the waltz movement than a romantic rubato in the style of Chopin.

H J-M What seems to me very unusual is to see the constant repetition of the words 'expressive' and 'very expressive' which stride through the piano score.

THIRD WALTZ

H J-M And the third waltz?

V P The difficulty in this third waltz is to isolate the third beat; this results in a hesitation before embarking on the first beat (Ex 48).

H J-M Yes, there we find the Viennese waltzes of Schubert in which Ravel sought his inspiration.

V P Here, as in the first waltz, the rhythmic accents are displaced (Ex 49). He was very keen on doing this.

The pedal is also very important in this waltz. It must help to bring out the rhythmical phrasing. After the double bar, the second episode must be played very melodically, and Ravel particularly wanted the short *diminuendo* which leads to the repetition of the phrase (see page seven, fourth line, third and following bars).

H J-M As we have often noted, there's a little comma which allows the pianist to resume the theme gracefully.

V P Gracefully is the word, since Ravel told me: "like a curtsey". The echo of this phrase is as if broken off. Ravel insisted so much on all this punctuation!

H J-M Moreover it is marked on the music!

V P Here (Ex 50), the interpretation of this passage poses an interesting problem in sonority. Ravel wanted the leading part 'expressive' as marked, with the upper part very sustained.

H J-M I have indeed noticed that the chords are often heard in clusters they have the same density.

V P The execution of the upper part always raises the problem of the inde pendence of the fingers.

H J-M It's the soprano part which sings. . . .

V P The passage marked 'very expressive' in the recapitulation must b played very romantically and freely (see page nine, third line, fourth an following bars).

H J-M And the end?

V P The final sounds must dissolve into a distant rhythm which foretell the rhythm of the next waltz.

H J-M One mustn't be afraid of letting the last note die away before goin on.

FOURTH WALTZ

V P As usual, Ravel wanted the swell hairpin well marked, but without an slowing down (Ex 51). The rhythm must not be weighed down as a result.

Here (Ex 52), the arpeggio must be sinuous but muscular.

J-M And again, you find the little comma which lets a breath of air in before the repeat.

P That is how Ravel asked me to play it, in fact. After the double bar, the theme of the waltz is more projected, as if amplified (see page ten, fourth line, fourth and following bars).

J-M Here it comes close to the great orchestral *Valse*! You told me about a personal modification which Ravel made to one waltz. Isn't it in this one?

P I see on my music, in his handwriting, the addition of an ascending phrase to the printed text, which enriches it in a singular way.

J-M What's more, it's the version which he chose for the orchestral score.

P And to finish, let's stress that Ravel was absolutely adamant about making the marked repeat.

J-M The last four waltzes date from 1910. They were much discussed at the time, their novel harmonies having startled the more conservative composers.

I would like to speak today about the ballet which arose out of these waltzes. The dancer Trouhanowa asked Ravel to orchestrate them for a ballet. Ravel, attracted by the idea that his waltzes would be danced to, wrote his own story-line. Thus was born 'Adélaïde' or 'Le Langage des Fleurs'. The ballet was performed at the Théâtre des Arts in 1912 in Drésa's delightful settings. In his fondness for the Restoration, Ravel had imagined a salon at the home of a beautiful coquette. The rococo furniture, the 'bouffe' hair-styles and the old-style clothes of the ladies bear witness to the period in which Ravel situated *Adélaïde* and this décor can give pianists an accurate idea of what I might venture to call the "good–bad taste" style intended by Ravel.

I won't tell you the story of the ballet; all you need to know is that it i
based on the language of flowers (hence the title): the red rose is th
emblem of passion, the poppy the flower of oblivion. . . . The poet Ren
Chalupt, in *Prétextes Littéraires*, wrote: "This floral symbolism which wa
widely cultivated in the Middle Ages is certainly in the spirit of Romanti
cism associated with Charles X, permeated with reminiscences of th
Gothic and the practices of chivalry. The fact remains that Ravel delighte
in affirming, through dance, the rather faded grace of these waltzes. W
said previously that he was inspired by the waltzes of Schubert, but adde
to the free fantasy of a Schubert is a feeling for the antiquated with whic
Ravel was fascinated, if only to contradict it slyly by some little discord.

Here are the movements:

Fifth waltz: *Presque lent dans un sentiment intime* (almost slow
intimately)

Sixth waltz: *Vif* (lively)

Seventh waltz: *Moins vif* (less lively)

Eighth waltz: *Epilogue – Lent* (Epilogue – slow)

FIFTH WALTZ

H J-M I see on your score: 'In the spirit of a waltz by Schubert'.

V P Yes, Ravel wrote that himself on my music.

H J-M It's probably the tender and intimate aspect of this waltz whic
dictated this comparison.

V P There is a tendency to play this waltz too quickly because of the walt
rhythm which persists in the bass. You must give the theme its sentiment
side.

H J-M Without having recourse to rubato, for all that!

V P Above all, not that! Ravel was very insistent on this point and marke
'simple' on my music (Ex 53).

H J-M And it's probably this simplicity which links it more to the waltzes of Schubert.

V P Here (Ex 54) in the passage marked *très fluide* by Ravel, a duple rhythm intervenes once again, but it must fit into the bar without any modification.

H J-M As so often with Ravel, the lyrical outpouring is in opposition to the play of the rhythms.

SIXTH WALTZ

H J-M And the sixth waltz?

V P An extremely difficult case presents itself here.

H J-M You scare me! What is it then?

V P It's the ever-present question of the opposition between duple and triple rhythm which marks out these waltzes! This particular 'one-legged' rhythm, as you call it, is particularly complicated because it is divided between the two hands (Ex 55). It's only possible in a rapid tempo; from that to playing it too hurriedly is only a step! But Ravel's *vif* is never hurried!

H J-M This lack of synchronisation between the hands must be devilishly hard!

V P And Ravel uses it a lot in his *Valses*!

H J-M With the perverse little smile of a conjuror!

V P It demands great independence between the hands.

H J-M One might also say it's an example for a Dalcroze eurythmics class!

V P This waltz rhythm is counted as one in a bar, as shown by the phrase marks, on to which is grafted the duple rhythm of the left hand, itself divided by a three-beat rhythm, and there you have it.

H J-M Don't you bring out the left hand rather a lot?

V P It's the only way to weld the passage together and bring it off as Ravel demanded.

H J-M Demanded?

V P Oh yes! It's probably the passage he made me repeat the most.

H J-M In any case, it will be interesting for future interpreters to know just how much importance Ravel attached to this problem. Tell me, isn't there another little rubato at the end of this passage?

V P 'Rubato' is a little exaggerated for Ravel. You just have to follow the printed markings to the letter: 'very soft and rather languid', which are sufficiently evocative, to my mind.

This same passage returns a second time and there the rubato no longer exists. Ravel wrote on my music: 'supple, but without slowing down' (Ex 56).

In the middle of this waltz there is a melodic line which must be sustained in spite of the contrary rhythms, and which ends with an echo effect (Ex 57).

H J-M And the end is an exact repeat of the opening of the waltz.

SEVENTH WALTZ

H J-M The beginning of the seventh waltz is preceded by a curious little preamble which is reminiscent of the yearning theme of the preceding waltz.

V P This preamble is also interesting in that Ravel wanted the repetition of these three arabesques to sound very different; the third should be languid.

H J-M Yes, the arabesque-reminiscence dies away in order to allow the short crescendo which follows to act as a springboard for the launch of the real theme of the *Valse* (Ex 58).

It seems to me to be the most Viennese of all the waltz themes.

V P You are right, and that's why you must bring out its character by stressing the swell and the staccato crotchet (Ex 59). Here (Ex 60), in addition to 'expressive' which is marked, Ravel wanted it to be, as he said, 'expansive'.

H J-M Undoubtedly the bashful and modest Ravel reveals his true nature in his Waltzes.

V P Here (Ex 61), the left hand not only stands out as marked, but is also incisive.

H J-M And the third beat must lift off 'à la Viennoise'. This great crescendo leads to the character of the great orchestral waltz. It's Vienna itself! And don't let's forget the big organ points! (see page 18, bar 3).

V P After this explosion the little interlude appears all the more refined (Ex 62).

H J-M I can hear some little discordant touches which must have disturbed the listeners of 1910!

V P And Ravel insisted that they should be brought out. Although it is marked 'very soft', he asked me to let the melody stand out here.

H J-M And we won't discuss again the play of duple and triple rhythms with which this waltz abounds.

V P The organ point at the end must be very long.

H J-M It is the end of the *Valses* in effect, since the last one is an epilogue.

EIGHTH WALTZ – EPILOGUE

H J-M We must take some time to explain the eighth waltz, this epilogue which clasps echoes of all the preceding waltzes to its bosom. . . . 'A Dream of Waltzes' is the name which could be given to these misty memories if the title had not been debased by a piece of light music. Yes . . . it is surely a dream; all these waltzes rising gradually out of the blurred memory seem to be reborn. Like all second flowerings they no longer have the strength to bloom completely . . . these are only snatches of waltzes . . . they mingle gracefully and a little regretfully, but they fit well together in the Epilogue, where, in spite of the diversity of themes, the magnificent unity of the piece reigns supreme.

V P I shall interrupt you here, for Ravel was so keen on this unity of rhythm that we must stress it. It is, moreover, one of the difficulties of interpretation of this waltz.

H J-M Can you give us some examples?

V P Here is the theme of the Epilogue (Ex 63a), and here it is with the sixth waltz (Ex 63b). Here is the Epilogue again with the fourth waltz (Ex 63c), and the evocation of the rhythm of the first (Ex 63d).

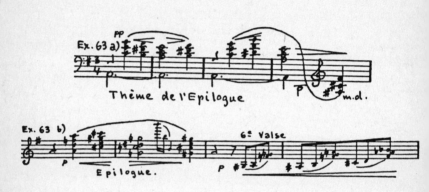

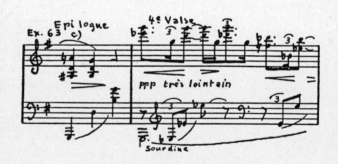

In no way must the beat change when the different rhythms of the scraps of waltzes appear.

H J-M In fact, as you have done to convince me, they can be played to the metronome!

V P Ravel wanted the epilogue to be slow whilst keeping its waltz rhythm. The grace notes, the ornaments, must not be fuzzy, even when played gently, and must fall very precisely on the beat (Ex 64).

H J-M There's always the same Ravelian strictness, yet in this waltz there is a marking which is unique in the work of the composer. The last time the theme of the Epilogue returns, Ravel has written: 'A little more wearily'.

V P Basically it's a kind of rallentando which he doesn't want to admit to, and which indicates the melancholy mood which prevails throughout the Epilogue.

H J-M Don't you find that the beautiful, sonorous phrase at the end is a tribute to the second Waltz, which is perhaps the most Ravelian?

V P In spite of the pianissimo marking, you mustn't be afraid of bringing out the melody of this admirable second Waltz (Ex 65).

MA MÈRE L'OYE
PRÉLUDE
A LA MANIÈRE DE . . .

H J-M Our session today will differ from the preceding ones in the sense that Vlado Perlemuter will not make any special comments on the works to be played: *Ma Mère l'Oye* (*Mother Goose* – children's pieces for piano duet) and *Prélude*. Although Ravel himself played *Mother Goose* with Perlemuter at a concert of the S.M.I., he never gave him any advice concerning this piece, which proves that he was well pleased with the interpretation. Full of admiration for Perrault's tales as well as those of Madame d'Aulnoy and Madame Beaumont, Ravel wanted to set them to music; he composed a suite for four hands, moderately easy so that his young friends Mimi and Jean Godebsky, to whom the work is dedicated, could play it as a duet.

This little masterpiece of simplicity will let you enter a realm where Ravel is king: that of the child's soul. Why? Because Ravel had retained the freshness of a child's impressions! Fairies, devils, imps, gnomes and fairy gardens were his world. To attempt to explain Ravel is impossible without bringing to light one of the most engaging aspects of his personality: Ravel had retained the joyful wonder of childhood, the capacity to admire and also the rather cruel unconcern which sometimes troubled his family and admirers. Yes, childhood had bequeathed him a taste for wonder: fairy tales, oriental tales, Greek mythology, fabulous poems inspired some of his most beautiful pages. How much at ease he feels in the unfathomable! With what illusionary scenery does he not surround the fairyland of *Mother Goose*! It is true that the orchestration adds even more magic to its chimerical sonorities. Composed in 1908, *Mother Goose* was performed at the S.M.I. in 1910 by two very little girls. In parentheses, and in order to show the musical richness of the time, in the programme, apart from *Mother Goose*, there was the first performance of Fauré's *Chanson d'Eve* and also *D'un cahier d'Esquisses* by Debussy, presented by Ravel at the piano. So you see, things were not too bad!

The two little girls who gave the first performance of *Mother Goose* at this concert were Jeanne Leleu (a pupil of Madame Long) and Geneviève Durony (a pupil of Madame Chéné). We are pleased to have one of them with us: Jeanne Leleu, who is going to play *Mother Goose* with Perlemuter; Jeanne Leleu who, after gaining the Premier Grand Prix de Rome, became a professor at the Conservatoire and the eminent composer whom we all know. I asked her what impressions she had of Ravel when she was a little girl; unfortunately, Jeanne Leleu is as modest as she is talented, so I am obliged to be her interpreter. "I found this great master so simple", she told me, "and I was also surprised when he asked us to play so simply, without looking for expression in every note! He wanted the first piece, the *Pavane*, to be very slow — for children that's quite difficult! He wanted the *Petit Poucet* to be very uniform in sonority. I used to wait impatiently for the cuckoo to enter! It was great fun to play the cuckoo! *Laideronnette* had to be very clear, like little crystal bells, without hurrying the melodic phrase in the bass.

"And what else?", I asked her. "Have you a characteristic memory of the rehearsal?". "Oh yes", she said, "I have a gory memory of *La Belle et la Bête*. There was a certain *glissando* which tore my finger. I hoped that Ravel would be more lenient than my teachers and would allow me to play the scale normally, without sliding, but when I showed him my bleeding finger, he simply said "I am an assassin!", but did not change the *glissando*!

For the ending of the piece, he asked the player of the lower part to use the pedal to put a halo round the chords of the first part. . . . He wanted *Le Jardin Féerique* to be very slow and sustained. This kind of music, so new to me, seemed magnificent!"

As I have told you, Jeanne Leleu is exceedingly modest. She doesn't want to tell you herself of Ravel's joy on hearing himself so splendidly interpreted by those two little girls, but after the concert she received a letter from Ravel, which for my part I find exceedingly rare. It is well known how much Ravel detested writing, and above all, how much the idea of complimenting his interpreters intimidated him; one always learnt that he was pleased through a third party! Here is the letter: "Mademoiselle, when you are a great virtuoso and I am an old man either crowned with honours or completely forgotten, perhaps you will have sweet memories of having obtained for a composer the very rare joy of hearing a rather special work interpreted with the exact feeling required. Thank you a thousand times for your child-like and spiritual performance of *Ma Mère l'Oye* and accept, Mademoiselle, the grateful feelings of yours sincerely, Maurice Ravel."

As we are concerned with Jeanne Leleu, we must mention the *Prélude*, which Ravel composed as a sight-reading test for the Concours de Piano, the competition in which the young pianist obtained a first prize. She read it so brilliantly that Ravel dedicated the little piece to her. He made this known in yet another letter, which I am going to read to you: "Mademoiselle, General Picquart has perhaps made you aware of my intention to dedicate to you the sight-reading piece, which Durand will publish under the title of *Prélude*. It's only a little thing: a souvenir from an artist who has been sincerely touched by your musical qualities. Continue to play like that, for yourself alone, without bothering about the public. Besides, it's the best way of getting its approval. Please remember me to your parents and believe, Mademoiselle, in my great artistic sympathy. Maurice Ravel."

"A little thing", said Ravel, but you will realise how recognisable Ravel's stamp is, even in "little things".

A LA MANIÉRE DE . . .

H J-M Before we undertake the study of the *Le Tombeau de Couperin*, Vlado Perlemuter will play two pieces by Ravel entitled: *In the manner of . . .*, which will be informative about Ravel's musical irony and also about his knowledge of the work of other composers. Before Ravel was involved in this game of pastiche, the pianist Alfredo Casella had already issued his first album entitled: *In the style of . . .*, in which he good-humouredly plagiarised Wagner, Debussy, Faure and others. Very amused at this new style, Ravel, as soon as he arrived at Casella's, sat down at the piano and caricatured all the music. One day, when he had succeeded particularly well in a pastiche of Chabrier pastiching Gounod, Casella begged him to write down his improvisation, so that it could appear in his second album; this he did. You are going to hear it, as well as a Waltz by Borodin which is really "an extract" from Borodin, apart from a little Ravelian resolution which glides past the ear.

Let's listen to *In the manner of Chabrier*, a paraphrase of an aria from *Faust* whose Chabrier–Ravel sevenths would have astonished Gounod! You will realise the extent to which Ravel knew his Chabrier!

LE TOMBEAU DE COUPERIN

Prelude
Fugue
Forlane
Rigaudon
Menuet
Toccata

H J-M *Le Tombeau de Couperin* dates from 1917. Ravel, after joining up as a soldier, falls ill. He is eventually discharged and feverishly starts to write music again. *Le Tombeau de Couperin* is the last thought which he will give to the war, each of its six pieces being dedicated to the memory of a friend fallen on the field of battle.

Ravel was criticised a great deal at the time for having written jolly music to honour dead friends. Personally, I feel quite differently about it; Ravel offered his music to his friends in the same spirit that the Juggler of Notre Dame offered his juggling to the Virgin Mary – by giving himself completely. Ravel's reticence in matters of sentiment is well known; words of affection left his lips with difficulty . . . But in music? Write music for his friends, that's what he could do! After this heartfelt impulse, what does it matter whether the music is sad or cheerful?

Ravel admired Couperin; the idea of being inspired by him was an homage to the French tradition; what's more, Ravel liked to yield to the constraints of a framework. . . . Didn't he say to his pupils, in this now famous sentence: "Copy, and if while copying, you remain yourself, that's because you have something to say". Ravel tried to copy Couperin . . . and produced Ravel!

Vlado, what, in your view, is the affinity with Couperin?

V P The clarity of the writing, first of all; the form of the Suite, the liveliness of expression and certain harmonic cadences. This clarity, moreover, necessitates an extremely clean technique to go with it.

H J-M Do you play it as if it were by Couperin?

V P No, I play it like it is by Ravel, but it goes without saying that the discipline which the composer has imposed on the form as much as in the writing, transmits itself quite naturally to the interpreter.

Prelude

H J-M What are your comments?

V P The beginning must be extremely clear. Very lively, but, as always in Ravel, without hurrying.

H J-M This unpedalled sound evokes the woodwinds of the orchestra.

V P This leads me to point out that Ravel asked for very sparing pedalling in this *Prelude*. You might say pedalling by little dabs.

Here (Ex 66), Ravel was particularly strict about the grace notes being played on the beat, in spite of the rapid tempo.

H J-M Moreover, this is marked at the foot of the score.

V P It's really very difficult.

H J-M Almost harpsichord writing.

V P Here (Ex 67), the outline must be very clear but one must not forget to colour the chromatic movement of the left hand.

H J-M This chromatic line has the effect of making the arabesques of the upper part more pliant.

V P You mentioned woodwind just now. Here (Ex 68), Ravel told me: "like an oboe".

Here (Ex 69), you have to accentuate the bass to sustain the consecutive fifths.

The same thing applies here (Ex 70). You must gently underline the little figure which is suddenly brought in as if to introduce a variation.

H J-M This gives a kind of melodic weight to the passage which might otherwise be heard differently. And at the end?

V P Ravel wanted pedal for the tremulo. The pedal should not be lifted on the final chord.

H J-M In this way, the big diminuendo fades out in the pedal. . . .

Fugue

H J-M Can you give us the elements of this *Fugue*?

V P Here are the subject and counter-subject (Ex 71):

Here are the subject in contrary motion and the counter-subject in contrary motion (Ex 72):

H J-M What strikes me about this *Fugue* is not only its rhythmic character but also the economy of its subject. There's daring for you! How much wealth was Ravel able to discover in just four notes!

V P Not to mention the rhythmic accentuation, which is very difficult for the interpreter, for it is not a brutal accent, but an expressive weighting which varies according to the intensity of the phrase. This kind of accentuation, which continues throughout the piece, calls for great independence of hands and fingers.

H J-M And it gives its character to the whole *Fugue*. In short, should this *Fugue* be played very simply?

V P Yes, but not academically; with a certain inner intensity. Note this passage (Ex 72), which, for the first time constitutes a dialogue between subject and counter-subject, both by direct and contrary motion.

H J-M Ravel was well versed in all the devices of fugue, even though he was refused the Prix de Rome! It is so easy to see Ravel, the craftsman, enthusing over all these mental gymnastics!

V P Mental gymnastics, but also from the heart. You must not be afraid of bringing out the intensely expressive character of these thematic combinations. I once heard this fugue played very romantically . . . too romantically, but I must admit that although I did not completely agree with the interpretation, it opened up new horizons for me!

H J-M To sum up, you certainly don't want this *Fugue* to be treated as an academic exercise.

V P No, for the expressive element is intense.

Forlane

H J-M Now let's consider the *Forlane*. I'm delighted to hear you play it on the piano, for the orchestral version has always disappointed me.

V P Why? The orchestration is delightful!

H J-M From the lesser to the greatest conductor, not one achieves the balanced rhythm of the *Forlane*. It's always fast and above all, skipping along.

V P But Ravel did not put any dot on his score, simply a slur. . . .

H J-M Vlado, play us the *Forlane* as Ravel asked you to play it. . . . Decidedly, I hear only curtsies and bows in this music, not skips.

V P Ravel asked me not to play the last quaver of the group too heavily (Ex 73); it makes only a tiny break before the second beat. There is only a shade of difference between that and making it sound like a grace note.

H J-M Don't you think that the staccato quaver of so many interpretations is only an exaggeration of what Ravel wanted? However, I have heard him sing the theme; it had pace, but was balanced and even a little melancholy . . . like a regret. . . .

V P It is, in fact, the piece in the *Tombeau* which most evokes the past, with its pastel tones and archaic cadences of which we have already spoken (Ex 74).

The continual modality is not without a certain monotony (see page twelve, line 2, bar four, and line three, bar one), yet Ravel insisted on all the repeats. Here (see page twelve, line three), we must mention again the grace notes being played on the beat.

H J-M Isn't there a passage where the theme should really be treated more cheerfully than at the beginning?

V P Yes, the new episode which recalls the opening theme (Ex 75) is, unlike it, detached and above all, very accentuated, with its answering phrase very soft, like a reply.

H J-M And the end?

V P The end very much like a musical box (Ex 76).

Ravel asked me to observe carefully the difference between the two similar phrases, of which the second is an echo of the first – and not to slow down! (Ex 77).

H J-M We know how attracted Ravel was to dance tunes; minuets, pavanes, a forlane, a rigaudon and waltzes inspired some of his most beautiful pages. Even in the chamber music dance themes can be found; the *Blues* of the *Sonata* for violin and piano, and even the great *largos* of the *Trio* and the *Duo* for violin and 'cello could be assimilated into noble sarabandes. As for his works inspired by Spain, they nearly all arise from the dance. Ravel is Basque . . . this inclination for dance rhythms is one of the characteristic features of the Basques, and I think it is in the Basque soil that one must dig to find the roots which bind Ravel so particularly to the dance. Moreover the imposed form was a limitation – and Ravel liked limitations so much! No one knew better than he how to yield to the form whilst keeping his own personal hallmark.

Rigaudon

The triumphant opening of the *Rigaudon* seems like a noble salutation before the dance!

V P The most delicate thing, in this piece, is to make the figure in the bass stand out, but discreetly, in the continuous rhythm of the rigaudon (Ex 78).

H J-M This musical-box continuity is one of the most important elements of the piece.

V P The rhythm is continuous, but the sonority must vary. Thus in this passage (Ex 79), Ravel asked for a brassy sound.

H J-M He also assigned this passage to trumpets in the orchestration of the *Rigaudon*.

V P In the *Rigaudon*, as in other pieces in the *Tombeau*, the pedal must be used with a lot of tact, underlining both the rhythmic aspect and the harmonic aspect.

Here (Ex 80), despite the pianissimo indicated by Ravel, the fact that he wanted me to imitate the oboe proves that he wanted a penetrating sound, all the more so because the following episode must be played with a mysterious, thin sonority, in a distant pianissimo (see page 18, line 1).

H J-M And the melody, rather melancholy and so typical of Ravel – how did he want it played?

V P He wanted it played without any shading; the continuity of the melody is enough in itself. He was equally insistent on maintaining the bass rhythm throughout this episode (Ex 81).

H J-M It is obvious that lyricism would spoil the bearing of the phrase!

V P Exterior lyricism! For one has to play it with great inner expression. Ravel did not want the end of this episode to slow down. However, one must give it a certain flexibility so that the last note dies away before the initial theme is brought back.

H J-M It's amusing to note that the repeat of the theme, which could have been only a simple *da capo*, is embellished with a modulation which is really a surprise element (Ex 82).

Menuet

H J-M Among the old dances, the minuet attracted Ravel above all. His first work is the *Menuet Antique*, whose mediaeval mode evokes the *Menuet Pompeux* of Chabrier. The second minuet is the one built on the name of Haydn, but the most 'Ravelian' one is that of the *Sonatine*. There Ravel gives his attention less to the form than to the capricious modulations which bring him incomparable freedom of composition; modulations, moreover, which bring him back discreetly to the key of the piece. The minuet from *Le Tombeau de Couperin*, the last one, is less elaborate. It is, however, enriched by a *musette*, but the mould of a Couperin minuet encloses it more rigorously. It adheres closely to the form, although all spirit of pastiche is absent.

H J-M Will you let us know what Ravel suggested to you?

V P This piece must be played at a going pace, not making it too heavy and always placing the grace notes on the beat.

H J-M If one is not careful, this piece can sound monotonous. How do you vary the colour?

V P Through the intensity of sound in certain fragments. Thus the second couplet is much more melodic than the beginning of the movement, in spite of the pianissimo marked (Ex 83).

H J-M It's almost nostalgic. . . .

V P Here (Ex 84), many pianists diminuendo on the third beat, whereas Ravel asked for a continuous crescendo.

H J-M Once again, one has to seek one's own interpretation in accordance with the exact indications of the composer.

V P Ravel asked me to play the *Musette* in the same tempo and give a lot of breadth to the following episode (see page 21, line 3).

H J-M The repeat of the first theme of the *Menuet* must slot into the *Musette* without jarring – all the more reason for keeping the same speed. And here we are at the coda.

V P There is much to say about the end. Here (Ex 85), one must play with calm expression and without changing the speed.

Here (Ex 86), is a kind of recitative in tempo in which the intensity erupts and subsides on just two notes.

H J-M The end is extremely 'Ravelian', with its cat-like spring which brings back the rhythm of the *Minuet*.

V P Ah! that charming effect! (see page 23, line 4, bar 3.) In fact, Ravel wanted it to be quick and unexpected, like a surprise after the three crystalline chords which precede it (Ex 87). These chords should be played strictly in time. Above all, follow Ravel's marking and let the trill die in the pedal (see the last three bars).

Toccata

H J-M Ravel liked to criticise his own works with serene objectivity. . . .
thus he liked to demonstrate to us that the ending of his *Toccata* was pure
Saint-Saëns! What do you think, Vlado?

V P I think there is a little bit of truth in this paradox, especially as it
concerns the piano writing.

H J-M This piece is really dazzling as far as piano technique is concerned.
Did Ravel give you any special instructions?

V P I have few indications from Ravel for this *Toccata*, apart from emphasising the rhythmic side and playing it as clearly as possible. It is really
written for its virtuosity and should be played as such.

H J-M As in *Tzigane* where Ravel piles on the difficulties for us violinists.
He was knowledgeable about all instruments and his greatest joy was to
exploit them to their fullest extent. Did you know that before writing
Tzigane, he made me come to Montfort to play Paganini's twenty-four
Caprices to him? He wanted to outdo the devil!

V P If, too often for my liking, this *Toccata* is played at a diabolical speed,
I must admit that Ravel wanted it quite fast. In the episode which is a little
less lively (see page 26, line 1), Ravel really slowed down. He asked me to
play it expressively and sustained without dragging, then returning, as
marked, to the original tempo

H J-M But the second theme is also very expressive?

V P Oh yes! All the more so because it must dominate the rhythm of the toccata, which from then on becomes a veritable *perpetuum mobile* (see page 27, line 3 etc).

H J-M It seems to me that a rather feverish dialogue is established between the two themes?

V P And Ravel was very fond of this dialogue. That's why one must not exaggerate the speed, which removes its clarity.

H J-M Obviously, you must let it breathe, so that the rhythm of the toccata can remain clear and detached from the intense melodic line.

V P Ravel asked me to allow both parts time to express themselves, both the toccata and the expressive melody (Ex 88).

Here (Ex 89), Ravel asked me to start piano, with the soft pedal, in order to prepare carefully for the crescendo. Piano, but intense. When the first episode is repeated in its outburst of alternating rhythmic chords, Ravel asked me to take it a little slower in order to make the accents felt, gradually resuming the initial tempo, but without giving the impression of a gallop! (See page 31, line four, fifth and following bars.)

H J-M And would you play for us the finale, which Ravel insisted was pure Saint-Saëns!

V P Here it is (Ex 90).

H J-M Thank you Perlemuter, and thank you also for reviving for us, with such integrity, the wishes of our dear and great Ravel.

CONCERTO IN G MAJOR
CONCERTO FOR THE LEFT HAND

Pierre Maylan Together with the *Concerto in G*, the *Concerto for the left hand* is Ravel's last great work; he was then aged 55. Before succumbing to apraxia, an illness paralysing all creative impulses, he wrote only the three songs: *Don Quichotte à Dulcinée*.

Ravel began his two piano concertos in the spring of 1930, completing them in the autumn of 1931. The one for the left hand was written at the request of the Austrian pianist Paul Wittgenstein, who had lost his right arm during the 1914–1918 war and was in search of a repertoire. Ravel said that he composed this concerto in such a way "that it gives the illusion of being written for two hands". He achieved this illusion thanks to the use of an extraordinary range of technical refinements put at the service of a bubbling invention and an astonishing sense of timbre and rhythm.

In an interview given to the *Daily Telegraph*, Ravel said: "The *Concerto for the left hand alone* is quite different from the other in character. It has a single movement with many jazz effects and the writing is not so simple. In a work of this nature, the important thing is not to give so much the impression of a light texture, but that of a part written for two hands. Therefore I have used a style much closer to the usual style of the traditional concerto. After a first section full of this feeling, there appears an episode in the character of an improvisation, which gives way to a piece of jazz. It is only from what follows that one realises that the jazz episode is actually constructed out of themes from the first section."

It is possible that Ravel introduced jazz elements into this work following attacks from the avant-garde, who were beginning to treat him as a reactionary. Already at the time of 'Les Six' – with whom Arthur Honegger fell out on this point – and with their lively approval, Erik Satie had written an article in which he said: "M. Ravel refuses the Légion d'Honneur, but all his music accepts it."

From its first performance this concerto has inspired enthusiasm. Roland-Manuel wrote: "This piece, full of fever and dash, is invested with the magic of an incantation. It restores to life with new sorceries, the fantastic people of *Gaspard de la Nuit* and the poetic bestiary of *Histoires Naturelles*. The orchestra has a completely new sound, now dull and gloomy, now dry and brutal, occasionally shot through with flashes of fire."

Maître, did you have an opportunity to talk to Ravel about this concerto?

V P I didn't have the opportunity to see Ravel again after 1929, the year in which I played all his solo piano works in two recitals, after studying them with him. I knew, however, through Roland-Manuel and Hélène Jourdan-Morhange, that there had been many clashes between Ravel and Wittgenstein over this concerto, to the extent that Ravel had removed the first performance from him and it was first played in Paris by Jacques Fevrier. Ravel had been put out, indeed offended, by the changes which Wittgenstein, to whom the work is dedicated, had made in his editing, even in its actual composition, to the extent of altering whole passages.*

P M Are there any particular technical difficulties in this concerto?

V P There are two difficulties: the large stretches and the leaps. This demands a very broad hand, especially in the progression of chords at the beginning of the first cadenza. As in *Le Gibet*, certain chords, elevenths and tenths, pose a problem for many pianists. (See fig 4 in the score.) But whereas in *Le Gibet* the very character of the passage excludes the least idea of an arpeggiando – besides, Ravel was against it – it is possible in the *Concerto* not to play blocked chords but to spread them. I am thinking for example of the eleventh: G sharp–C sharp (Ex 91).

P M What tempo do you take in the *Lento*?

V P You must follow Ravel's indication: 44 to the crotchet, which sometimes is not done by some young pianists who take this movement too fast. Using his intuition Ravel solved the melodic problem, posed by the fact that there is only one hand, by playing the top note of the chord with the thumb, which is strong and carries more weight from the hand. Paradoxically, it would be more difficult to play this concerto with two hands; you wouldn't achieve the same expressive unity.

P M It's often difficult to hear the melody, swamped as it is by excessive pedalling.

V P The use of the pedal is complicated here. You have to use half-

*Paul Wittgenstein played the Concerto at the Saltzburg Festival in 1936, under the baton of Arthur Rodzinsky. The critics deplored the brutal and violent character of the interpretation, with its excessive contrasts conforming so little to the spirit of the work.

pedalling, or vibrato pedalling, as often in Debussy's music, to avoid harmonies overlapping or mingling.

Ex. 91

P M How do you conceive the *Allegro*, which according to certain interpreters, often becomes a cavalcade devoid of expression?

V P In my opinion Ravel's markings must be followed. He indicated 138 for the dotted crotchet; on no account must you exceed 144. In the second theme of the *allegro*, already played in the first movement by the horns and which makes you think of a blues, the rhythm is more intense, more tragic. Played too quickly, this theme, repeated by the bassoons and trombones, and which is a prelude to the final piano cadenza, cannot be given all its depth if the speed is too fast. Too often the orchestral accompaniment is weak. At figure 28, these are not simple *pizzicati*, but dotted notes in the violas and 'cellos, which sometimes lack rhythmic nervosity (Ex 92).

P M Have you any advice to give about fingering?

V P As there is only one hand, it isn't possible to give many alternatives. In the *Allegro*, I recommend some fingerings which make for robustness, but they are awkward. Take for example, the main theme of the *Allegro* (Ex 93):

You will notice that I use the thumb as much as possible, even in passages which are not merely melodic. In this case I found the fingering which allows the rhythmic profile of the passage to be underlined.

P M Does the printed score conform to the original?

V P Yes, but I would like to draw your attention to a printing error in the final cadenza (Ex 94):

The 'A' in the bass must be repeated. Ravel forgot to remove an extra leger line at the change of clef, so that the 'A' of the bass clef becomes F sharp, which alters the fundamental bass.

P M Ernest Ansermet writes that the *Concerto in G* is the most important work of Ravel's last years. What do you think of this opinion?

V P Performed for the first time in Paris on 14 January 1932 with Marguerite Long at the piano and the composer conducting, the same interpreters then toured this work around central Europe with immense success. other hand, the *Concerto in G*, for which arrangements had been made as to the date and interpreter for its first performance, found him 'pawing the ground', especially in the *Adagio*, which caused him real agony of mind.

PIANO CONCERTO IN G MAJOR

P M Performed for the first time in Paris on 14 January 1932 with Marguerite Long at the piano and the composer conducting, the same interpreters then toured this work around central Europe with immense success.

Ravel wrote about it: "This concerto, which I propose to perform myself, is a concerto in the strictest sense of the term and written in the spirit of those of Mozart and Saint-Saëns. Indeed, I think that the music of a concerto can be bright and brilliant without claiming to be profound or aiming at dramatic effects. It has been said of certain great classical composers that their concertos are conceived not so much *for* the piano as *against* it. For my part, I consider this criticism to be perfectly justified. At first I intended to call my work: 'Divertissement', then I decided that there was no need, as the title: 'Concerto' is sufficiently explicit, taking into account the character of the music. In certain respects my *Concerto* is not unlike my *Violin Sonata*; it uses some jazz elements, but only in moderation. . . ."

Conceived in three movements, two quick ones surrounding an *adagio*, this concerto makes a revolutionary contribution to Ravel's works, inasmuch as, apart from the jazz allusions, the composer constantly uses bimodal and polytonal superimpositions. Only the *Trois Poèmes de Mallarmé* show more audacity. In the two fast movements the orchestral writing is extremely subtle. Ravel brings to the fore brass and woodwind instruments which play as soloists, even bassoons and horns, and he uses a vast array of percussion instruments. In the first movement there is perpetual exuberance, a feeling of jubilation in which the piano participates, adding its particular timbre to the orchestral colours, but this ardour is interrupted from time to time by contemplative sequences, such as the one developed by the clarinet and muted trumpet passing from major to minor as in a blues, or the one presenting a lyrical theme interrupted by staccato chords. The last movement is a kind of *toccata* in which the piano constantly responds to the orchestra with brilliant virtuosity and overflowing joy.

The central movement, *Adagio assai*, has given rise to a host of commentaries. It is a *cantilena* of thirty-five bars, developed by the piano alone then eventually surrounded by dry dissonances from the orchestra, which seems to be frightened of this tonal, almost diatonic melody. Over a persistent triple-time rhythm, this marvellously simple melody seems to have poured out spontaneously, but Ravel confessed that he had taken infinite trouble to write it, saying one day to Marguerite Long: "I did it two bars at a time, with the help of Mozart's *Clarinet Quintet*".

Referring to this piece, Ernest Ansermet recalls the *Boléro*, claiming that, as in that masterpiece, it is not the melody which determines the speed, but the speed which controls the melody. With this difference: in the *Boléro* there is a single theme repeated unrelentingly, whereas in this *Adagio* the melody, conditioned by the uniform rhythm, is released in a series of calm outpourings.

FIRST MOVEMENT: *Allegramente*

P M What advice do you have about the speed?

V P *Allegramente* does not mean *presto*! One must take into account avel's marking: 116 to the minim. If you play it too quickly you lose wind nstruments and the whole display of the piccolo. The repeat is often taken oo fast (fig 10 in the score), to the detriment of clarity and neatness. The erformance of the pianist is affected by this and becomes strained. The ame applies to the *Finale*.

ECOND MOVEMENT: *Adagio assai*

M Marguerite Long discovered how difficult it is to sustain the intense xpression of this melody at such a slow speed. Shouldn't you accelerate omewhat the tempo which Ravel had in mind?

P If need be you can take it at 80 instead of the 76 to the quaver as narked by the composer. It's a case where the personality and feeling of he interpreter is involved. On the other hand, when the cor anglais epeats the theme, you must play it at 76 so that this instrument can xpress itself with ease.

M Is there a similarity between this *Adagio* and Mozart's *Clarinet Quintet*?

P The similarity resides in the fact that Ravel uses the instruments as oloists. Sometimes this intention of Ravel is not understood. The brass and voodwind must not be afraid of 'playing out'.

M When the melody is repeated by the orchestra, how should the piano mbellishments be played?

P The piano decoration is a melodic counterpoint and not a simple xercise in composition. You must clothe the basic melody in all its finery. would like to draw attention to the quality of legato in this magnificent age. A certain amount of rubato may be allowed if it is performed taste- ully, as Marguerite Long did at each repeat of the decorative passage.

M Fauré is often mentioned in connection with this movement.

P Rather than thinking about the *Clarinet Quintet* of Mozart, it can be aid that Fauré is often present in certain passages. Here is an example layed by the flute (Ex 95):

Fl.

The same can be said of the phrase which follows, repeated by the obo
and the cor anglais.

THIRD MOVEMENT: *Presto*

P M What speed do you recommend?

V P Ravel did not give a metronome marking. Was this deliberate? On
thing appears to me to be important: the rhythmic pulse must be a quicl
two, so the time-unit must be a crotchet, not a minim. 144–152 to th
crotchet seems to me to be the speed to recommend. The theme at th
beginning reminds me of a toccata, particularly the one in the *Le Tombea*
de Couperin (Ex 96).

Ex. 96

The influence of jazz technique is most noticeable in the trombon
chromaticisms.

P M Doesn't this concerto, which is so different from the one for the lef
hand, appear to be less Ravelian in its conception and feeling?

V P On the contrary, it's like Ravel in its fantasy, charm and instrumenta
colour. He creates a lighter atmosphere, save in the admirable *Adagio*
where I believe the longest phrase in the whole of Ravel can be found
exceeding in its thirty-five bars the great melody of *La Vallée des cloches*
which consists of only twenty bars.

I would like to add that in my opinion the first movement is the most complicated to interpret. In this movement the rhythmic first theme contrasts with the *meno vivo* (fig 4 in the score), which must be played very flexibly, even *poco rubato*, without, however, upsetting the unity of the sequence.

In the cadenza another difficulty is the trill (fig 26 in the score), which must resonate in a singing, even manner. In the second part of the cadenza one must try to imitate an instrument which no longer exists: the musical saw, used at the time of *Le Boeuf sur le toit*, and used in jazz during the same epoch.* Ravel marks exactly the notes which you must use for the trills and the little chromaticisms acting as links between the trills (Ex 97).

Ex. 97

*In his *Etudes* (Editions Claude Avenline, Paris, p 84), Darius Milhaud describes the method of using the musical saw: ". . . you place the handle of the saw on your right knee and hold the end of the blade with the left hand, bending it to a greater or lesser extent to increase or decrease the vibration, which you obtain by beating the centre of the blade with a kettle-drum stick. Once the blade is set in motion, the movement of the hand modifies the pitch, and the most beautiful melodies escape from its invisible throat. New Orpheus, thus would you tame the ears of even the greatest infidels, those who are most deaf to anything new." The musical saw was fashionable in about 1918; one still came across it around 1930.

(*Editor's note*: Milhaud's description is not quite accurate. The saw handle must be gripped between the knees. The pitch is controlled by the extent to which the blade is bent by the left hand, and the amount of vibration is determined by the force of the beating, or in most cases, by the force of the bowing, for the saw was more often played with a violin-bow than with a kettle-drum stick. The two features of the musical saw were its pure, unearthly sound and its continuous glissando, of which the Ondes Martenot provides the modern equivalent. It was not a specially constructed instrument but an ordinary saw.)

At figure 27 (Ex 98), I would like to draw attention to the fact that the right hand, supported by the violins, must be more sonorous than the left hand, as if developing and bringing out a very lyrical melody.

P M The critic and composer, Gustave Samazeuilh, claimed that Ravel cut several bars from this phrase once he had completed the work, judging that he had over-developed it.

V P This assertion could well be true; Ravel was not fond of excessively long passages. Moreover, this characteristic of his style is a contributory factor to the beauty and enduring nature of his work, whose qualities we have endeavoured to reveal through the advice on interpretation given in this book, which we hope will be a help to musicians, both present and future.